Me and my Body

DK

DK | Penguin Random House

Designer Polly Appleton
Editor Hélène Hilton
US Senior editor Shannon Beatty
Fact checker Wendy Horobin
Photographer Ruth Jenkinson
Producer John Casey
Producer, Pre-Production Nadine King
Jacket designer Amy Keast
Jacket coordinator Francesca Young
Managing editor Penny Smith
Managing art editor Mabel Chan
Art director Jane Bull
Publisher Mary Ling

First American Edition, 2018
Published in the United States by DK Publishing,
a division of Penguin Random House LLC
1745 Broadway, 20th Floor, New York, NY 10019

Copyright © 2018 Dorling Kindersley Limited
24 25 26 10 9 8 7 6
011–308132–Feb/2018

A catalog record for this book is available
from the Library of Congress.
ISBN: 978-1-4654-6866-6

DK books are available at special discounts when purchased in bulk
for sales promotions, premiums, fund-raising, or educational use.
For details, contact: DK Publishing Special Markets,
1745 Broadway, 20th Floor, New York, NY 10019
SpecialSales@dk.com

Printed in China

All images © Dorling Kindersley Limited

www.dk.com

MIX
Paper | Supporting
responsible forestry
FSC™ C018179

This book was made with Forest
Stewardship Council™ certified
paper—one small step in DK's
commitment to a sustainable future.
Learn more at
www.dk.com/uk/information/sustainability

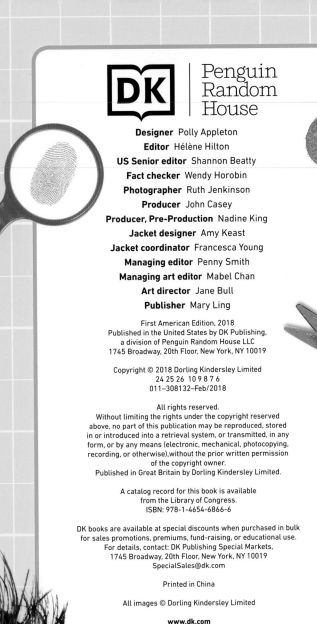

Parents

This book is packed with
activities for little ones to enjoy.
All projects are designed to be
done with adult supervision.
Please be safe and sensible—
especially when you're doing
anything that might be
dangerous (or messy!)
Have fun.

Contents

You are super!

We all have the **same** **body parts**, but there are some things that **make** us different from one another.

Did you Know?

You are a perfect mixture of your mom and dad. They both passed on some of their features, such as hair or eye color, to make you one of a kind.

Head

Ear

Hair

Eye

Mouth

Neck

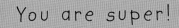

Some body parts come in pairs, such as hands, legs, ears, and eyes. You have only one heart, brain, and liver.

No matter how you look, your body is amazing!

Fingers

Arm

Shoulder

Elbow

Hand

Chest

Tummy

Toes

Nose

Leg

Knee

Foot

Teeth

You are covered in skin from head to toe.

Team work

Your body parts all work together as a team to keep you going. Many body parts are hidden away inside you, but they're really important, too.

5

Building a person

Your **body** is **made** of very **simple** stuff, but put it all together and it makes something amazing—**you!**

Did you know?

Every human body is made up of trillions of cells.

Atoms

Atoms are the smallest things in the universe. They join together to make molecules, such as water.

Cells

Molecules make cells. Cells are the building blocks of all living things. There are more than 200 different types of cells in a human.

Tissues

When the same type of cells stick together they form tissues, such as skin, fat, or muscle.

Cells

Body cells are so small they can only be seen under a microscope. Every type looks different because they all do different jobs. Nerve cells are long and thin, while skin cells are flat.

It's a person!

Your body relies on every cell, organ, and system to work as a team to keep you alive.

Organs

Systems

Organs are made of different types of tissue. Each organ has a job to do. For example, your liver's job is to clean your blood.

Organs work together in groups called systems. There are many different systems in your body. One of them is your digestive system, which takes nutrients from food to power your cells.

Did you know?

Everything in the whole universe is made up of atoms. Even you!

See me grow

Your **body** changes throughout your life. It all starts **inside** your mom's tummy.

You started life as a teeny tiny cell, smaller than a period.

Everyone is born as a **baby** ...

1

Babies are born after growing for nine months in their mom's tummy.

Children have lots of growing and learning to do.

2

then grows into a **child** ...

8

What's a belly button?

In your mom's tummy, you were joined to her by the umbilical cord. It gave you food and oxygen until you were born. Your belly button is where your umbilical cord used to be.

Teenagers are changing from a child into an adult.

Adults are fully grown people.

3

4

then into a **teenager**...

and finally, an **adult.**

9

Family tree

Make your unique **family tree** to show you with all your relatives.

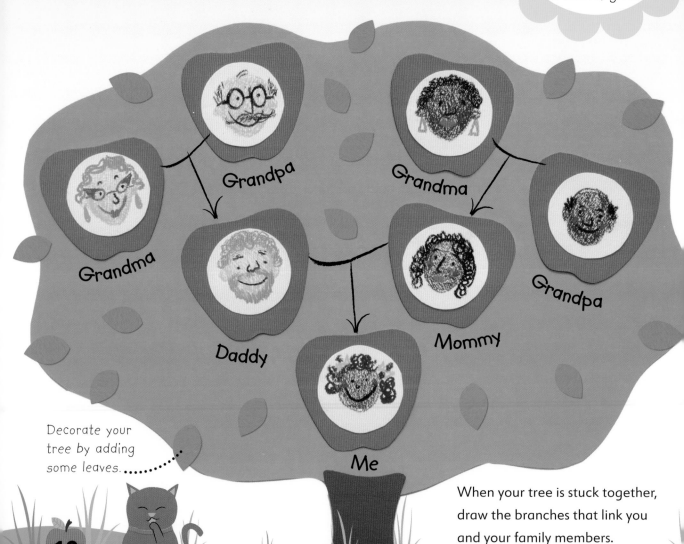

Grandpa

Grandma

Grandma

Grandpa

Grandma

Daddy

Mommy

Me

Decorate your tree by adding some leaves.

When your tree is stuck together, draw the branches that link you and your family members.

1

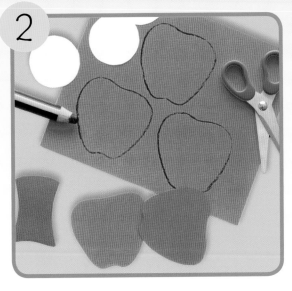

Draw a tree shape that is big enough to fit all your family members. Ask an adult to cut it out.

2

Draw a tree trunk, apple shapes, and white circles. Ask an adult to cut out all the shapes.

3

Draw pictures of all your family members. Add special features, such as glasses, eye colors, and hairstyles.

4

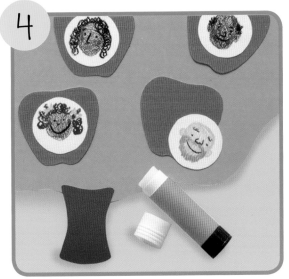

Glue the trunk to the bottom of the tree. Stick the faces onto the apples, then glue them onto the tree.

Touchy feely

Your **skin** is covered in tiny **sensors,** called **nerve** cells, that help you feel things.

Warm and soft

How do you feel?

When you touch something, the nerve cells in your skin send a message to your brain to tell you how it feels. Different types of nerves can feel different things.

Under your skin

Surface of skin

Texture sensor

Upper skin layer

Light touch sensor

Pain sensor

Lower layer

Firm pressure sensor

Vibration sensor

Fat

What happens to your skin when you take a long bath?

Fingerprints

The skin on your fingertips is covered in little lines. This pattern is your fingerprint. No one else in the whole world has the same fingerprints as you.

Look closely

Is your fingerprint...

an arch?

or a loop?

or a whorl?

Try it out

Print your fingertips using colorful inks. What pattern do your fingerprints make?

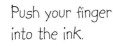

I

Ink pad

Push your finger into the ink.

Did you know?

Your skin color is unique, just like your fingerprint. You get your skin color from your parents. Sunshine makes it get darker.

Decorate your prints with felt-tip markers...

and googly eyes.

2

Paper

Print your finger onto paper.

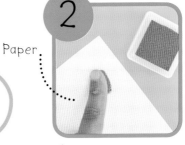

13

Special senses

Your **senses** tell you about the world **around you**.

Look!

Your eyes help you see. Light comes in through your pupil and hits nerves at the back of your eyeball. These tell your brain the shape and color of an object.

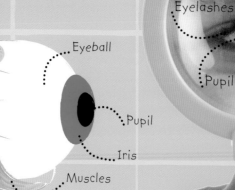

Eyebrow

Eyelid

Eyelashes

Tear duct

Pupil

Iris

Eyeball

Pupil

Iris

Muscles

Optic nerve

The optic nerve sends information about what you can see to your brain.

Eyebrows, eyelashes, and eyelids protect the eyes from germs, dust, water, and sunlight.

Listen!

Your ears let you hear sounds. Sounds are little vibrations in the air. The vibrations pass along your ear canal to nerve cells that tell your brain what sounds you are hearing.

Look inside your ear

Cochlea

Eardrum

Ear canal

Bones

Taste buds recognize five tastes: sweet, sour, salty, bitter, and umami (savory).

The three little bones in your ear are the smallest in your body.

Outer ear

Tongue bumps

Taste!

The tiny bumps on your tongue contain taste buds. They help tell you what food tastes like.

Smell!

Your nose can smell around one trillion different scents. It helps your taste buds to taste your food.

Did you know:

Your ears also help your balance. They tell your brain which way is up and how fast you're moving.

15

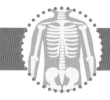
Super skeleton

Inside your body are lots of hard **bones.** These **bones** make up your **skeleton.**

Your bones are super-strong and hard. Without your skeleton you'd be soft like jelly.

Bony armor

Some bones protect your inner organs. Your skull is like a hard helmet for your brain. Your ribs protect your heart and lungs.

Skull

Ribs

Arm

Spine

Hip

Helmet

Hand and finger bones

Thighbone

Kneecap

Shinbone

Feet and toe bones

Seeing bones

You can't see your skeleton from the outside. Doctors take x-rays to see bones inside your body.

Try it out

Clench your fist and flex your arm to see your muscles pulling on your bones.

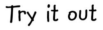

This muscle pulls on your forearm to bend it up.

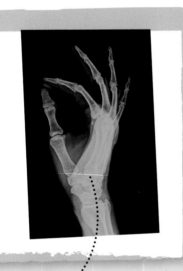

X-ray of a hand.

Joints are where bones meet.

This muscle relaxes.

Most animals have skeletons

Not me!

Ready, set, go!

Muscles are attached to your bones. They work in pairs to pull on your bones and make them move. When one muscle pulls, the other relaxes.

My body map

Now you've seen some of your **insides**, you can make a **map** of your own **body**!

Use a different color for each organ so you can tell them apart.

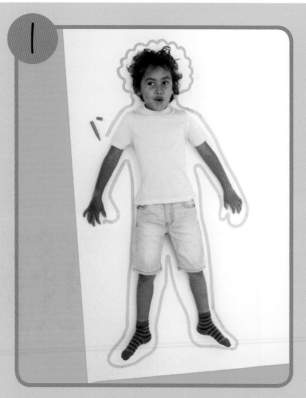

1

Unroll the paper and lie down on it. Ask a friend to draw around your body.

2

With your pens, draw on your eyes, mouth, nose, ears, and brain.

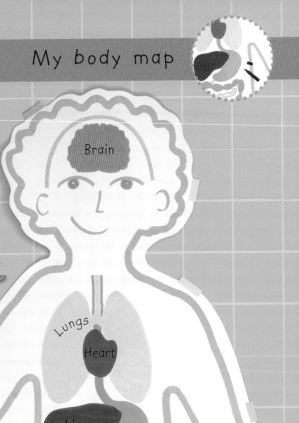

Did you Know?

Your largest organ is your skin. It completely covers you to protect you from water, germs, and sun.

4 Carefully cut out your body map and hang it up.

Brain

Lungs

Heart

Liver

Stomach

Intestines

Bladder...

You can label your organs if you like.

3

Look at the diagram above to see where to draw your heart, lungs, liver, stomach, intestines, and bladder.

Your smart brain

Your **brain** is your body's control room. It does all your **thinking** and learning, and tells your other body parts **what to do.**

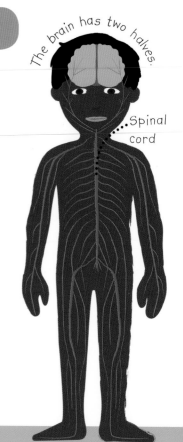

The brain has two halves.

Spinal cord

Nerves send signals to your brain from all over your body. The signals travel up the spinal cord in your backbone to your brain.

Human brains contain 100 billion nerve cells.

This is what brain cells look like through a microscope.

Did you know?

There are more than 400 miles (650 kilometers) of blood vessels in your brain.

Your brain is wrinkled up so that it can fit inside your skull.

20

Your brain controls everything you do.

At five years old, your brain is 90 percent of its adult size.

You tell your muscles to move here.

Touch signals arrive here.

This area does lots of thinking and imagining.

This part lets you talk.

Hello!

This is where you understand words.

Sight signals come here.

Sound signals arrive here.

The cerebellum helps you move and balance.

The brain stem controls things that you don't think about, like breathing.

Learning

New brain cell connections are created as you learn. The more connections you grow, the easier it becomes to do something.

21

Amazing blood

Your **blood** is your body's delivery system. It carries everything that your **organs** and cells need to work.

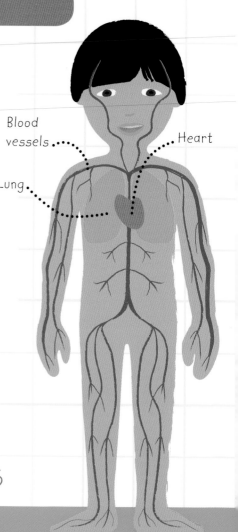

Blood vessels......

Heart

Lung.

What's in your blood?

White blood cells help your body fight off germs.

Red blood cells carry oxygen to cells and organs.

Plasma makes blood runny and delivers nutrients where they are needed.

Sticky platelets stop you bleeding if you have a cut.

Did you know?

Blood is mostly made of clear plasma, but blood cells make it look red.

22

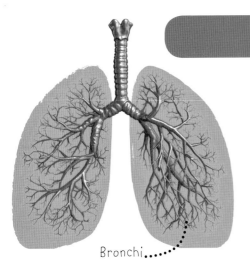

Bronchi

Your lungs

You breathe air in with your lungs. Bronchi are tiny tubes that take oxygen from the air to your red blood cells.

Your heart

Your heart is a strong muscle. It works hard to pump blood around your body. It never takes a break!

Can you feel your heart beating?

Blood is pumped to the lungs to get oxygen.

Blood with oxygen is pushed out to the body.

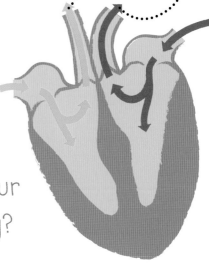

Try it out

Your heart pumps 10½ pints (5 liters) of blood around your body every minute. See how hard it works.

Fill a bowl with 10½ pints (5 liters) of water.

Use a small cup to tip the water into a second bowl. Phew! It's hard work.

Time one minute on a clock.

23

Paper lungs

Your **lungs** **breathe** air **in** and **out.** Make these paper lungs and watch them **expand** as they **fill** with **air** from your lungs.

You will need:
Sponge
Pink or red paint
2 paper bags
2 flexible straws
Tape

Real lungs are full of tubes and little pouches that move air in and out. This makes them feel soft and spongy.

1

Dip the sponge in pink paint and print the spongy pattern all over the paper bags.

2

Bend the straws as shown and tape them together just above the flexible part.

3

When the paint is dry, tape a bag to each straw just below the crinkly bend.

4

Blow in and out of the bags through the straws to see how the paper lungs get bigger and smaller.

The pouches in your lungs are called alveoli. They pull oxygen into the blood and push carbon dioxide out.

Yummy food

Your body needs lots of **energy** to work and grow. All your energy comes from **food.**

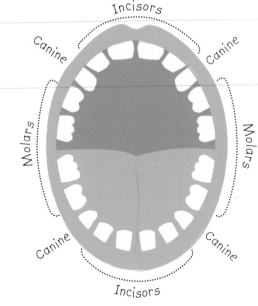

Different types of teeth do different jobs. Incisors cut food, canines rip food, and molars crush it.

Starchy foods, such as bread, pasta, and rice give you lots of energy.

Fruit and vegetables are full of fiber and vitamins.

What should you eat?

Different types of food have different nutrients. That's why it's important to eat a balanced diet.

Proteins, such as meat, eggs, and beans make your cells healthy.

You also need healthy fats, found in foods such as avocados and nuts.

Milk, cheese, and yogurt are full of calcium that makes your bones strong.

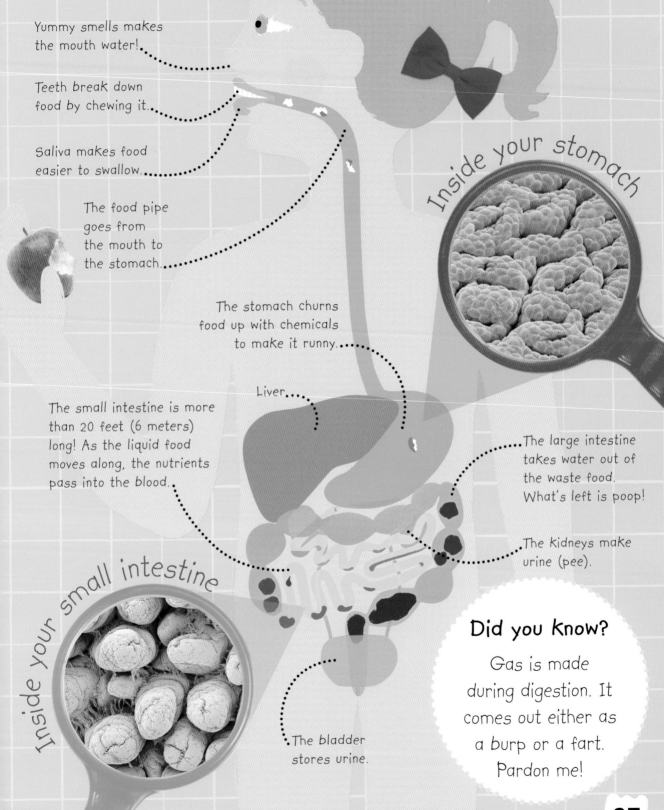

Yummy smells makes the mouth water!

Teeth break down food by chewing it.

Saliva makes food easier to swallow.

The food pipe goes from the mouth to the stomach.

The stomach churns food up with chemicals to make it runny.

Liver.

The small intestine is more than 20 feet (6 meters) long! As the liquid food moves along, the nutrients pass into the blood.

Inside your small intestine

Inside your stomach

The large intestine takes water out of the waste food. What's left is poop!

The kidneys make urine (pee).

The bladder stores urine.

Did you Know?

Gas is made during digestion. It comes out either as a burp or a fart. Pardon me!

27

Germ attack!

Germs are tiny little things that attack your body and can make you sick. Luckily your body has very **special** defenses to help you fight back.

Doctor

If you do get sick, a doctor can often give you medicine to help you get better.

Viruses are the smallest type of germ. They give you colds and other diseases.

Bacteria are single-celled organisms. An upset tummy is often caused by bacteria you've eaten.

Parasites steal their food from another animal's body. Tapeworms live in the gut.

Your body is full of useful **bacteria** that live in your gut and break down food.

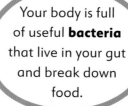

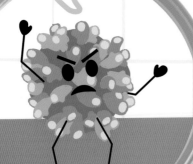

Types of germs

Not all germs are the same. There are many different types—some are bad for you, and others are helpful.

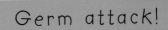

Try it out

Make pretend germs by putting glitter on your hands. Can you wash them off?

You can't see real germs on your hands! But you can wash them off with soap and water.

Skin

Your skin is like a tough shield. Germs can't get through it unless you have a cut.

Macrophages hunt down germs and gobble them up.

Lymphocytes poison germs or tell macrophages where germs are.

Neutrophils rush to a cut to stop germs entering your body.

Defense squad

These special white blood cells help your body fight back against nasty germs!

Stay healthy

You are completely unique and special! It's really important that you learn how to **take care** of yourself.

Exercise

Human bodies need to move. Exercise makes your muscles, heart, and even your brain healthier.

Did you Know?

Around a third of what you eat should be fruit and vegetables.

Food is fuel for the body. Your body needs the right amount of different foods to stay fit and healthy.

Yoga

Dance

Jump rope

Run

Bike

Walk

Have fun as you exercise!

30

Hug

Laugh

Create

Learn

Read

Keep your brain happy!

Talk

ZZZZZZ

Your body and brain need sleep to recover from the day. Children need around 10 to 12 hours of sleep every night.

Happy mind

Taking care of yourself doesn't just mean looking after your body. Your mind needs to be happy too! Tell people you trust when you don't feel happy so that they can help you.

Did you know?

Some illnesses affect the brain and can change how someone feels. These are called mental illnesses.

31

Index

Acknowledgments

The publisher would like to thank the following for their kind permission to reproduce their photographs:

(Key: a-above; b-below/bottom; c-center; f-far; l-left; r-right; t-top)
123RF.com: 5second 12c, Andrey Kiselev 15cl, Danila00 23tl, Deyan Georgiev 14clb, Dmitry Kalinovsky 14cl (Macro eye), Eric Isselee 17bl, Juan Gaertner 20cla, Karel Joseph Noppe Brooks 2bl, 31bc, Keerati Thanitthitianant 12b, Lafoto 9crb, Leung Cho Pan 9clb, Monthian Ritchan-ad 17cl, Mrdoomits 16cb, Nanette Grebe 7c, Oksana Kuzmina 12cla, 30c, Pahham 17cr, Pavel Losevsky 14cla, Rawpixel 4–5b, Sergey Galushko 14cl, Shojiro Ishihara 15c; Alamy Stock Photo: D. Hurst 26clb, Rosemary Calvert 3br, 15clb; Depositphotos Inc: Bilanol.i.ua 12bc; Dreamstime.com: Goncharuk Maksym / Photomaks 26crb, Pogonici 26cb; Fotolia: Nito 16cl; Science Photo Library: Steve Gschmeissner 27clb, Susumu Nishinaga 27cra.
Cover images: Front: 123RF.com: Rawpixel cla; Fotolia: Nito cb; Back: 123RF.com: Oksana Kuzmina clb.

All other images © Dorling Kindersley

DK would also like to thank Carrie Love for editorial assistance.

Bye

Bye